SURREY

A portrait in colour

ANDY WILLIAMS
with text by Graham Collyer

PRESENTED BY

LILLY RESEARCH CENTRE

First published 1992
© Andy Williams 1992
Revised 1999
This presentation edition published 1999

COUNTRYSIDE BOOKS
3 CATHERINE ROAD
NEWBURY, BERKSHIRE

Cover design by Mon Mohan
Produced through MRM Associates Ltd., Reading
Printed in Singapore

Contents

Lilly Research Centre
Erl Wood Manor – Windlesham

Eli Lilly and Company is one of the world's leading pharmaceutical companies and is committed to creating and delivering superior health care solutions.

Eli Lilly and Company set up its research facility at Erl Wood Manor in 1967. Since then the Lilly Research Centre has become a centre of excellence in neuroscience research, its scientists dedicated to the unravelling of some of the mysteries of central nervous system (CNS) disorders. Our greatest success to date has been the discovery of olanzapine, which was launched in 1996 and has proved to be a major advance in the treatment of schizophrenia.

Patent protection for these novel compounds is essential and the Erl Wood Patent Department works to secure and maximise the patent life of these and other Lilly products throughout Europe and the rest of the world.

Erl Wood is also a major business centre for Eli Lilly and Company in Europe. The clinical pharmacology and medical groups co-ordinate many aspects of worldwide clinical drug development from the first time an experimental compound is given to man through to commercialisation. It is the home of Eli Lilly European Regulatory Team responsible for obtaining regulatory approval in Europe for our highly successful medicines. The post-marketing support of a new medicine is provided through the Marketing, Quality Assurance and 3rd Party Manufacturing groups based at the site. At the same time, experts in pharmacovigilance and epidemiology ensure that the company's standards of excellence in medicine provision are upheld during the life cycle of every product.

Introduction

Any Portrait of Surrey is a subjective one. But there can also be objectivity. Andy Williams and Graham Collyer set out to show the beauty of this small but densely populated county from the west beside the Hampshire border to the east where it meets Kent, and from the northern edge with Berkshire and Greater London down to the rural south overlooking Sussex.

It is a county of contrasts, divided into 11 districts whose headquarters are uniquely and, contentiously, outside of the administrative area. County Hall is in the Royal Borough of Kingston upon Thames which, of course, was once in Surrey, as was much of suburbia right up to the Thames. Surrey has shrunk over the years, but England's greatest river still runs through part of the county thanks to boundary changes a quarter of a century ago.

Surrey is not what it was in William Cobbett's day, less still than when John Evelyn and John Aubrey were around and setting down their thoughts and discoveries. These three wise men knew the county as a land of agriculture and cottage industries and self-contained communities. It is a county dominated by the great roads from London to the south coast, with the Portsmouth Road (A3)

the most important. This route carved its way right across the county in a diagonal line through the great towns of Kingston and Guildford, over the wild moorland of Hindhead and on through Hampshire to Portsmouth. It is still the most important trunk road in Surrey, but now there are motorways – more miles of motorway, in fact, than in any other county. The M25 cuts a swathe through the top of the county, while the M3 sweeps across the north west segment and the M23 runs north to south and provides a fast link with the country's second airport at Gatwick which, although just in West Sussex, dominates the everyday lives of a large area of Surrey.

Modern methods of communications have changed the face of Surrey. No longer is it essentially a rural area with a handful of key towns where people went to work if their living was not derived from the land or from some locally-based industry. Now it is a fast-moving region dictated to by the needs of its inhabitants, where work increasingly takes them to London and even abroad.

Towns and villages have become dormitories for the capital which can be reached in well under an hour from centres like Guildford and Woking. The county is home to one million people, and the need for additional housing is threatening more of the countryside. The green belt has been under attack for more than three decades as developers seek to buy up parcels of land, and the county council's structure plan for the opening years of the new century, along with the borough and district plans, are put under severe pressure.

Nevertheless, Surrey is still a county of great landscape beauty as this book demonstrates. Much of the open space is owned by the National Trust or the local authorities and is available for everyone to use and enjoy. What is at risk is the land which acts as a buffer between the residential areas and the countryside.

The recession of recent years did slow down the house building programme, but now Surrey's green field sites are under threat again. Most at risk will be the part of the county inside the M25 as developers seek to win permission to continue the urban sprawl out from Kingston and Surbiton along the A3 corridor.

To the south of London's orbital motorway, Surrey also has to be on its guard for while the phenomenon of constructing golf courses on redundant farm land has all but disappeared, developers searching for disused agricultural land on which to build houses are exercising the minds of local planners.

So, Surrey's face has changed from that of the 1980s, but not nearly so dramatically from that of earlier decades. Aubrey, Evelyn and Cobbett faithfully recorded what they saw before the industrial revolution, and then Eric Parker, the doyen of Surrey writers in the last 100 years, brought a new dimension to setting down what he discovered and knew of the county. Their books are a wonderful history of how it was, and form the basis of any new work, but they would all be shocked, and perhaps saddened, at the way in which Surrey has had to come to terms with the modern age so dominated by the motor vehicle and materialism.

But the camera does not lie, and if they had this book before them they would see that Surrey still has leafy lanes, sleepy villages, busy market towns; and surely the views from the North Downs still remain as breathtaking as they were when they were alive to enjoy them.

Graham Collyer
Hindhead, 1999

Farnham, Castle Street

This is without doubt one of the grandest thoroughfares in the whole of the country. And sitting proudly and loftily above it all is the castle. For centuries the seat of the Bishops of Winchester, the castle is now the Centre for International Briefing, but the grounds and the keep are open to the public. Castle Street, whichever way you look at it, has tremendous appeal. The fine Georgian houses are a delight to the eye, and its width gives it a special grandeur. It is just a pity that too often a traffic tailback, waiting to enter the town's one-way system, spoils the view.

Farnham, the birthplace of William Cobbett, fell victim to some questionable architecture in the 1960s – did not every town? – but was not damaged beyond repair, and now much good work is taking place and it can hold its head high again. In the past Farnham was home to two men, Charles Borelli and Harold Falkner, who cared desperately for the place, and their work and influence live on and are enthusiastically advocated by the present day guardians of good taste.

Walks around Farnham are revealing. Narrow alleys reach out from the main streets and lead into courtyards where an upwards glance often brings a rewarding view of roofs and chimneys. The parish church is one of the biggest in Surrey and its 16th century tower is impressive. On the banks of the Wey is the Maltings, once a hive of industry when Farnham was surrounded by hop fields, but now an arts and cultural centre.

Hindhead

The Devil's Punch Bowl at Hindhead was one of the first tracts of land to come into the ownership of the National Trust, because when the common land on either side of the Portsmouth Road was put up for sale in 1904, following the death by suicide of its owner, Whitaker Wright, a financier who had been sent to prison for fraud, there was a risk that it might fall into the hands of developers.

Local and national opposition was such, however, that sufficient funds were raised to enable the land to be purchased and then offered to the fledgling National Trust which, since its formation in 1895, had focused its attention on buildings rather than open spaces. The handover was completed in 1906, and since then the Devil's Punch Bowl and the neighbouring Gibbet Hill have been managed, along with other land in the vicinity, by a local committee of the trust.

The Devil's Punch Bowl used to be called Highcombe, or Heccomb, Bottom, while Gibbet Hill was Butterwedge until the now celebrated murder in September, 1786, when a man, believed to be a sailor, but who has never been named, was robbed and killed by three men he had met and befriended on the road to Portsmouth. The four had imbibed in the old Red Lion at Thursley before setting off on the lonely slog over Hindhead. The unknown man was attacked and left for dead, but soon after the alarm was raised the three villains were apprehended, eventually sentenced to death and left to hang in chains on a gibbet on the top of Hindhead. Their bodies were suspended beside the old turnpike road for three years until a winter storm brought them crashing down.

Hindhead and its common has become something of a *cause celebre* as the Government seeks to find an alternative route for the A3. It is a problem that has exercised minds since before the Second World War, but it appears that a solution is as far away as ever. The situation has become more focused in the last decade as first one route and then others have been put forward. Now it has developed into a battle between, on the one side, supporters of a tunnel under Gibbet Hill and Tyndall's Wood, given in memory of Prof John Tyndall, the man credited with founding modern Hindhead in the 1880s, and, on the other, proponents of a new overland route. Meanwhile, the heart of Hindhead at the traffic-clogged crossroads has all but died.

Haslemere

Haslemere, a quiet but nevertheless influential little town deep in south west Surrey near to where the county shares a common boundary with both West Sussex and Hampshire, was first mentioned in the 13th century, when a market was granted to the Bishop of Salisbury. However, it was not until 1859, when the railway arrived, that it noticeably grew in size and population. Haslemere is on the Waterloo to Portsmouth line, and the building of the station was a major reason why great Victorians such as Tennyson, George Eliot, Sir Arthur Conan Doyle and George Bernard Shaw came to live in the area.

Tennyson's home was at Aldworth, high up on Blackdown, the West Sussex range of hills that protect the town from the south; Eliot was at neighbouring Shottermill; while Conan Doyle and Shaw were up the hill at Hindhead. These literary giants, and other contemporaries, wrote some of their great works in the area.

Haslemere nestles in a sheltered valley and has always been, in many ways, cut off from the rest of the county. Because of this it has had an independent spirit which exists to this day. Two centuries before a local architect, Inigo Triggs, designed the war memorial in 1921, the site at the top of the wide High Street was the butchers' shambles, and until the dawn of the 20th century a twice-yearly cattle market and fair was held there. At the opposite end of the High Street is the celebrated and important educational museum which was founded by Sir Jonathan Hutchinson in 1888 and has been on its present site since 1926.

Tilford

A timeless scene in south west Surrey. The eastern bridge at Tilford carries traffic over the River Wey just below the spot where it is joined by the Till or, as it is popularly referred to, the southern branch of the Wey. The single-carriageway bridge was believed to have been built by the monks at nearby Waverley Abbey, and closely resembles the western bridge whose beauty has for half a century been spoilt by a temporary structure put up by the Army as a wartime measure to bring traffic into the village. A few years back there was a propsal to replace that purpose-built but ugly bridge with a new one upstream of the ancient crossing, but regrettably the idea fell a victim to budgetary cutbacks. Tilford attracts thousands of visitors every year, simply because it has one of southern England's most perfectly shaped village greens which the cricket club uses as its home ground. On all sides of the triangle there is much of interest: Lutyens designed the village institute which also doubles as the cricket pavilion; the Barley Mow has been dispensing beer for 200 years; Oak Cottage was the home of William 'Silver Billy' Beldham, the great cricketer from the late 18th and early 19th centuries who played many times for England and died in 1862 when he was 96; and the great oak tree was beloved of William Cobbett who, in 1822, said it was the finest tree he had ever seen. Sadly, it is now but a shadow of its former self. And then there are the two rivers, the Till which flows in from the west, having bubbled into life up on the slopes of West Sussex's Blackdown, and the Wey, which comes in from Farnham and whose chalky birthplace is in the Hampshire countryside close to Alton. Canoeists paddle, children splash and riders stop to allow their mounts to quench their thirst. All three can take place in one happy group on a summer's day. And all the time, on any weekend from April to October, there is cricket, a scene that has not changed for more than 100 years.

Elstead Mill

It is often stated as fact that the mill at Elstead was recorded in the Domesday Book. It was not, but there is a strong possibility that it was one of the six mentioned as being in the Farnham Hundred which were held by the Bishop of Winchester when the survey was undertaken in 1086. The original building burnt down in the 17th century, soon after the second Civil War when Cromwell's troops were encamped there. When at last it was rebuilt it served as a working mill in a variety of guises until a little more than 100 years ago when Thomas Appleton employed 55 people in the manufacture of military braid and other accessories for soldiers' uniforms.

Since those days the mill has been a residence for among others the village policeman, and two great names in the motoring world: Chaplin Court Treat, who completed a legendary drive from the Cape to Cairo via the Sahara, when the motor car was still young, and H M Bentley, whose brother, W O, was the founder of the famous car bearing the family name. Now it is a restaurant and after some years as Bentleys it has reverted to its true name of Elstead Mill.

The impressive building straddles the mill stream which rejoins the River Wey at Elstead's old and traffic-threatened bridge, and then flows on through water meadows towards Godalming. The village, growing but still with its compact green and pleasantly grouped houses, was once dependent on wool – hence the names of two of its pubs, the Woolpack and the Golden Fleece – and carrot growing, the sandy soil producing some bumper crops.

Thursley

Attractive cottages and colourful gardens abound in Thursley, the small village in which Sir Edwin Lutyens was born and knew so well. His home was in The Street, close to where our photograph opposite was taken. The road leads from the pocket handkerchief sized village green, known as The Clump, to the church of St Michael and All Angels, and then on to the Devil's Punch Bowl, the National Trust wilderness that is mostly associated with Hindhead although it is in the parish of Thursley.

In the churchyard, which has far-reaching views to the Hog's Back across the environmentally important Thursley Common, the

visitor can easily find the stone that marks the grave of the so-called unknown sailor who was murdered as he walked over the summit of Hindhead on the night of September 24, 1786 (see page 10). The three men who were found guilty of the crime were sentenced to death and hanged in chains on Gibbet Hill close to the spot where the killing took place. The eagle-eyed in the churchyard will also spot the grave of Richard Court, the Thursley blacksmith who made the chains which held the bodies of Edward Lonegon, Michael Casey and James Marshall.

The neighbouring parish of Witley lies mainly to the east of the A3 and includes valuable common land owned by the National Trust. Witley village was favoured by the Victorian artists Helen Allingham and Myles Birket Foster, and the latter was buried in the churchyard close to the much-photographed Step Cottage shown here. The whole area around Thursley and Witley is rural but with quick connections to both the A3 and the main Waterloo to Portsmouth railway line. For the walker, there is a network of paths across the commons, but the lanes around the hamlets of Bowlhead Green and Brook offer relief from sand, heather and conifers.

The Hog's Back

Whether you travel east or west across the Hog's Back, the view is superb. The Hog's Back is a chalky spine – part of the North Downs – between Farnham and Guildford. It carries the A31 and is entirely dual carriageway, but before modern-day traffic demands made this a necessity, the road was quite narrow for a busy spur off the London to Portsmouth A3. Villages and hamlets nestle on either side; mostly they are now homes for people who earn their living elsewhere but, still, places like Puttenham and Seale on the south side, and Wanborough, to the north, are settlements where the past is ever-present.

The view to the south from the Hog's Back is of farmland and hills. The fertile fields in the valley of the River Wey between Puttenham and Milford give way to the heaths of Thursley and the hills of Hindhead with, as a backdrop, the heights of Sussex and the South Downs masking a still more distant Channel. To the north, it is a flatter vista altogether. The vast expanses of Pirbright Common and Bagshot Heath will be known, if not remembered with any fondness, by generations of training soldiers, while to the north east Woking's skyscraper office block sticks out like a sore thumb in a landscape whose distant discernible features are of the urban sprawl to the west of London and around Heathrow plus the towering buildings in London's Dockland.

To most, the Hog's Back is merely a fast road between two towns, but for those who care to stop at the large parking area on the south side above Puttenham or, better still, are energetic enough to walk up its slopes to the summit which, at 505ft above sea level, is one of Surrey's higher points, the scenery can be very rewarding indeed. The North Downs Way, which starts in Farnham, follows a course through Seale and Puttenham in the lee of the Hog's Back on its way to Compton and Guildford.

Chiddingfold

The best known of the Fold villages tucked away in the south west corner of the county, Chiddingfold has so many attractive angles. The view opposite, from across the pond to the parish church, is unusual. Photographers tend to concentrate on the Crown Inn, which is across the main road from the church, or the large village green with its forge at one end and solid houses round about.

The centre of the village offers picture postcard scenes, but residents and visitors alike must put up with heavy traffic on the Petworth Road. The church of St Mary has traces of the 13th century under a Victorian restoration, while the Crown, although altered many times, retains much to convince its customers that it was serving the needs of the village 700 years ago as well.

Bonfire night in Chiddingfold is a tradition which has been handed down for 150 years, and shows no sign of burning itself out. The fire on the green stands 30ft high and is lit by flaming torches which are carried in procession through the village. The organisers work hard for weeks to make the event, which attracts 10,000 visitors, a success, thereby ensuring that local elderly folk benefit from the proceeds at Christmas. It is a high-spirited celebration of one of the country's enduring anniversaries which, in 1929, did not have such a peaceful build-up. Then, 250 police officers were drafted into the village after the fire had been lit prematurely, and a Justice of the Peace was prepared to read the Riot Act.

Pirbright

Cricket on the green at Pirbright is one of the weekend attractions in this village to the north west of Guildford. Visitors come to enjoy the peace of the place, and relax around the green where, if you do not like cricket, the ducks – no pun intended – on the pond are a source of constant amusement to young and old alike.

Surrey has a number of village greens on which cricket is played, but in Pirbright they have been playing the game longer than in most other communities in the county.

A short walk from the green at Pirbright is St Michael's Church, where the graveyard is the last resting place of Henry Morton Stanley, an American explorer who completed many notable achievements in his life, which ended in 1901, but none more lasting than his utterance of the words 'Dr Livingstone, I presume' when he found the Scottish explorer on the shores of Lake Tanganyika in 1871.

While Stanley's memorial is a large upright piece of Dartmoor granite, those to Lord and Lady Pirbright, who were great benefactors to the village, are bound up in the history of the monarchy. A drinking fountain on the green was given by the couple to mark Queen Victoria's diamond jubilee in 1897; the village hall was a gift in 1899; and the recreation ground was completed two years later to celebrate King Edward VII's accession.

Godalming

The town's best known landmark is undoubtedly the Pepperpot (some people refer to it as the Pepperbox) and it has stood on its High Street site, guarding the entrance to Church Street, since 1814 when it replaced a medieval town hall. When traffic choked Godalming and movement at the Pepperpot came to a standstill, the awkwardly placed building was cursed for getting in the way, but few people have ever been prepared to campaign for its demolition or removal.

For decades it was the seat of local authority, and more recently the town museum (now resited across the road in more spacious surroundings). Now that a relief road has removed through traffic, the lovely old High Street is beginning to show off its finer points again. The town is looked down on, in the nicest possible way, by Charterhouse, the great early 17th century public school which came out of London in 1872, and whose buildings were constructed in the main using local Bargate stone. Carthusians who have made their mark around the world all came to know the charm of Godalming.

Away from Charterhouse, the town has had many famous sons, among them General James Oglethorpe, who founded the American state of Georgia in 1732.

In this century Jack Phillips became a hero when he remained at his post in the wireless operation room as the new super liner, the *Titanic*, struck icebergs and sank in the Atlantic Ocean in April, 1912.

Gertrude Jekyll, the celebrated Victorian gardener, lived at Munstead in the leafy southern part of Godalming, and her grave

can be found in the churchyard at nearby Busbridge. Miss Jekyll would have known the view shown on this page – the parish church of SS Peter and Paul across the riverside meadows known as the Lammas Lands – and what is especially noteworthy about the scene is that it has not changed demonstrably since those Jekyll days.

Winkworth Arboretum

Thousands of visitors find great enjoyment and contentment at Winkworth Arboretum. It was given to the National Trust in the 1950s, and is its only arboretum. The 99 acres are ranged over a natural hillside which descends to two lakes. Winkworth, close to Godalming and closer still to the attractive village of Hascombe, is a paradise for gardeners and walkers, but it was not always so. When the donor of the land, Dr Wilfrid Fox, first knew the place it was covered by hazel scrub and not unlike many another hillside in the district.

Dr Fox, senior consultant at St George's Hospital in London and a foremost figure in the specialisation of dermatology, moved to Winkworth Farm in 1938 without knowing anything significant about gardening. But he was a quick learner, and when, in the same year, the adjoining hillside covering 60 acres became available for purchase, he snapped it up. The fact that he was on holiday in Austria at the time did not hinder the sale.

He and a woodman transformed the rough acres into one of the finest collections of trees and shrubs anywhere in the British Isles. The azalea glade, modelled on a garden close to Lake Como in Italy, which Fox knew and loved, came first and other areas then just fell into place. In 1952, 14 years after he bought the land, Dr Fox gave it to the National Trust which, five years later, bought nearly 40 acres more.

The photograph inset on this page is of the White Hart Inn at nearby Witley. It was built as a hunting lodge for Richard II in 1381; his badge was a white hart.

Virginia Water

The Duke of Cumberland, having defeated Bonnie Prince Charlie at Culloden in 1746, returned to England and turned his attention to gentler pursuits. With his secretary, Thomas Sandby, who, somewhat handily, was an architect, engineer and landscape gardener, the Butcher of Culloden set about transforming an expanse of marshy and boggy ground in Windsor Park, of which the duke had become the ranger. With Sandby's skill they designed a park that attracts thousands of visitors every year.

Later in the 18th century the lake was enlarged so that it was about two miles long and covered 120 acres, big enough indeed for George IV to feel the need to have a small frigate built to sail on it. The vessel was still around during Queen Victoria's reign, and on one occasion a crew of a lieutenant and six sailors took it across the water to fire a royal salute from its cannon.

Virginia Water, because of its close proximity to Windsor, has always been known to royalty, and in 1816 the Prince Regent was presented with ancient Roman remains from Leptis Magna near Tripoli. At first they were considered suitable for the portico at the British Museum, but then the focus turned to Virginia Water and 10 years after being brought to this country they became a feature of this somewhat unusual corner of Surrey close to the border with Berkshire.

The University of Surrey

The University of Surrey moved to Guildford in 1968 – on to a purpose-built campus on a green field site on Stag Hill beside the still relatively new Cathedral. It was born out of the Battersea College of Technology, but its arrival in the county town, or at least on Stag Hill, was not wholly accepted. Objectors wanted it sited elsewhere, but there were powerful supporters, including the dean of the Cathedral and the editor of the *Surrey Advertiser*, whose leader columns frequently campaigned for the move to Guildford. The university was officially established by Royal Charter in 1966, and two years later 1,000 students moved in. Early forecasts were for as many as 5,000 students, but this figure has never been reached, and today there are in the region of 3,500, many of them from overseas.

In its first three decades, the university has, in spite of difficulties over funding, received worldwide acclaim for work across a wide spectrum of activities, particularly in the engineering and scientific fields. From the beginning, it set its sights on identifying the scientific needs of the remaining years of the 20th century, and beyond, and the need to establish a major research park. The present chancellor, the Duke of Kent, opened the park in 1986 and in spite of the recession early in the 1990s it has been able to attract major international and national companies to put down roots. The university is a centre of excellence and the mix of town and gown is important to the life and prosperity of Guildford.

Guildford Cathedral

Guildford's modern Cathedral of the Holy Spirit stands on Stag Hill, outside of the town, but so visible for many miles around. The illustration opposite shows the view from Bright Hill, just off the High Street, from where a panoramic aspect of Guildford catches the many moods of the county town.

From the laying of the foundation stone by the Archbishop of Canterbury on July 22, 1936, to its consecration on May 17, 1961, the cathedral slowly but surely took shape, and a generation of Guildfordians, living through the Second World War, watched its progress.

Clay excavated on the site when 800 piles were driven down 50ft provided the material for the bricks. The architect, Sir Edward Maufe, had definite ideas about the design and construction of a cathedral in a diocese that, he said, comprised no more typical English country, and he was determined that the building would express the heart of this beauty.

Whether in daylight or by floodlight, Maufe's vision in reality is confirmed. The cathedral is a bold and striking building, so different to the centuries old churches in other towns and cities whose names are perhaps more synonymous with the Anglican faith.

The land on which it was built was a gift from Lord Onslow, of Clandon Park, whose family name was and continues to be significant in so many aspects of life in Guildford. On another piece of open space once owned by the Onslows, stands a sport and leisure centre as fine as any in the country. Within sight of the cathedral, it will undoubtedly attract more people through its doors, but Maufe's magnificent work on Stag Hill will still be there long after the centre has outlived its usefulness and been replaced by the next state of the art design.

Guildford, High Street

So much has been written about the High Street in Guildford and its Guildhall and clock. But why not? They are gems. Taken for granted, perhaps, by local people, but beloved by visitors from around the world. Stand for a moment in the vicinity of the Guildhall on any day of the year and you will observe a camera lens being trained on this wonderful building whose front dates from 1683 but whose hall is Elizabethan and stands on an earlier structure. The clock was given by a London clockmaker, John Aylward, in return for the right to trade in the town.

The Guildhall has until comparatively recent times been both court room and council chamber, and indeed many civic engagements continue to be carried out there. It is a wonderfully atmospheric place, a civic treasure, whose custodian takes great pleasure in showing it off to visitors.

Guildford, the county town but alas not the seat of the county's administration, has a history dating back to Alfred the Great's time a little more than 1000 years ago, and was built where the river was shallow enough to be forded. The Normans constructed the castle, and the remains of the keep and outer walls, so close to the High Street, are popular attractions.

At the top of the High Street there is the 17th century Abbot's Hospital, together with a statue, which are reminders that an Archbishop of Canterbury, George Abbot, was born in the town; and across the road is the great 18th century Holy Trinity Church, once the cathedral church. Not far away stands the 16th century Royal Grammar School.

The River Wey

An idyllic scene on the Wey at Guildford. The river through the county town is part of the navigation owned by the National Trust between Godalming and Weybridge. Narrow boats and rowing boats can be hired from the Guildford Boat House, and holidays afloat from the town through to the Thames are popular.

The Wey cuts right through the heart of Guildford, and a towpath offers the opportunity for a pleasant walk, while the island opposite the boat house and the Jolly Farmer pub, whose gardens go down to the water's edge, is a pleasant place in which to just sit and relax.

Upstream, the navigation skirts the open expanse of Shalford Park and passes through St Catherine's Lock in the shadow of the ruined 14th century hilltop chapel of the same name. At Shalford, a pretty village of riverside cottages mixing with high-tech glass fronted office accommodation, there is the entrance to the long-disused Wey and Arun Canal.

Downstream, the river runs under Guildford's one-way traffic system and past the National Trust's offices at Dapdune Wharf, where barges were built in days gone by, and on under the A3 before at last reaching countryside again close to the refurbished Stoke Mill, now the home of the Surrey Advertiser Group of newspapers. The illustration on this page is of a footbridge over a quiet stretch of river near Burpham, only a mile or so from the town centre, and heading out towards the Elizabethan mansion at Sutton Place, and the stretch of water that was first made navigable by Sir Richard Weston in the mid-1600s.

Woking

The largest town in the county also has the tallest building. The British American Tobacco (BAT) office block can be seen from miles around, and as far afield as Guildford and the North Downs to the east and west of the county town. The centre of Woking is at

last no longer resembling a giant construction site, and the opening in 1992 of the Peacocks Centre was a bold move in the midst of a recession. At a cost of £120 million, it represented a massive investment and a huge slice of confidence in the eventual upturn in the economy. An all-embracing shopping and leisure development with an atrium bigger than any other in Europe, the Peacocks Centre was the latest step in the growth of the town that was built out of nothing, and alongside a village (now Old Woking), when the railway arrived in 1838.

Since those early Victorian days, Woking has grown not only upwards but outwards, and its environs encompass hitherto self-contained communities, unlike that of Goldsworth Park which at one time had the dubious title of Europe's largest housing estate.

The centre of Woking, though, is quite small, with the railway and station, from where passengers can connect to destinations throughout the country, and the Basingstoke Canal forming natural but vastly different boundaries. These two contrasting forms of transport, so close to the heart of one of England's most modern towns, provide a simple illustration of the short time-span in which Woking has developed.

Merrow Downs

Rudyard Kipling wrote about Merrow Downs, and if he were to return today he would find them little changed. The Downs have always had a special place in the hearts of Guildfordians, so close are they to the town. From the High Street it is no distance at all, although it is uphill, before you reach the grassy slopes at Pewley which take you on to the Downs.

In the 17th and 18th centuries, horse racing was held at Merrow. Huge crowds were attracted to the gallops, and King William III and King George I gave substantial prizes. The Whitsun week's racing was eagerly awaited and much followed, and Guildford traders cashed in. Interest eventually waned, however, but it was as late as 1870 when the last meeting took place, and by then Epsom and Ascot had taken over as the most popular venues. The old wooden grandstand which had stood on the Downs was demolished and burnt as Guildford celebrated November 5 one year.

Where horses raced, and cricketers played, for there was a fine ground at what was known as Merrow Basin when the game was still in its infancy, the golfers of the 113-year-old Guildford club have taken over. But you do not have to be a sporting type to enjoy the

Downs; the open space is available to all.

The illustration on this page shows horses at Gomshall, just over the hill from Merrow Downs.

Newlands Corner

The extensive area of open space on the North Downs at Newlands Corner, beside the A25 as it leaves Guildford and Merrow for Dorking, is one of those beauty spots that, like Box Hill to the east, attracts crowds of visitors whatever the weather. It is a superb spot to go to and blow the cobwebs away. In

winter, when there is snow about, it is a mecca for skiers and tobogganists.

Apart from the long-distance North Downs Way which crosses Newlands Corner, there are many other footpaths and bridleways for the rambler and rider to enjoy. Although most visitors prefer to arrive by car, Newlands Corner is best reached by foot or on horseback. From either east or west it is hilly, but the views are extensive and breathtaking. Coming from Guildford there is the little church on the top of St Martha's Hill at Chilworth which is well worth stopping at, and from the east the Silent Pool at Albury is a good starting place.

Newlands Corner made national headlines before the Second World War when Agatha Christie was thought to have gone missing there. A major manhunt by the police combed the woods and scrub after her car was discovered, but of the famous author of mysteries there was no sign. Eventually, she turned up in the north of England; her visit to Newlands Corner being part of a well planned false trail.

The illustration on this page is of the view from St Martha's which is on the route of the so-called Pilgrims' Way from Winchester to Canterbury.

Thorpe Park

This great leisure park is so untypical of Surrey, and yet it is undoubtedly the county's single most popular attraction. It opened in 1979 on the site of old gravel workings and in the intervening time has evolved into one of Europe's major theme parks with as many as 1.3 million visitors a year.

Planning regulations had required that the pits be refilled, but changes in the conditions were granted and work began on the 500-acre park in 1971, with the central theme being 'The History of the British People as a Maritime Nation'. The idea was for Thorpe Park to be an exhibition which brought together Britain's past with the latest in entertainment. The theme park concept was only just taking off.

When Lord Mountbatten opened the park a new era in entertaining the British family began, and the public response was overwhelming. Crowds flocked to this north west corner of the county, and soon there was a return on investment which allowed the owners to develop the park still further. The mid to late 1980s saw a change from the original concept and gradually the emphasis was put on public participation with the result that more and more people passed through the turnstiles.

Millions of pounds were spent on the new facilities as Thorpe Park met its competitors in a head to head battle for supremacy. Even in a recession, money continued to be spent by the management, and the old gravel pits, which could have taken 20 years to fill in, are still vying with the best of Europe's leisure grounds for the public's hard-earned cash.

Chertsey

The fine 18th century seven-arch stone bridge over the Thames at Chertsey is the only one of its kind in the county which is worthy of architectural merit. It has recently been restored and is on the site of a medieval crossing. Traffic heading out of the town over the bridge once entered Middlesex, but since the disappearance of that county and boundary changes the area north of the river is now in Surrey.

The Thames also separated the administrative districts of Westminster and Chertsey abbeys, with the exception that the Burway on the northern side at Laleham came under the jurisdiction of Chertsey which caused many an unholy squabble. Chertsey Abbey was one of the first to be established in the country, but do not expect to find much of it now. At the Dissolution it virtually disappeared and the stones were used in the construction of Hampton Court Palace. The abbey dated from the seventh century, was destroyed by the Danes in the ninth, and then rose again to be a power in the land.

One of its six bells survives and is rung in the parish church every evening. It is known as the Curfew Bell, but the legend associated with it is not based on any known fact. However, it is well documented and remains as one of the fascinating local tales that should be preserved for all times.

Chertsey town centre has some of the best preserved Georgian architecture in the county, and this has been complemented by some pleasing modern design. Sadly, though, the wall that Dickens had Oliver Twist climbing over to carry out his burglary was demolished not too long ago.

Sailing and boating on the Thames are popular pastimes and at Chertsey Reach there is the workshop of one of the finest oarmakers in the world, and also the base of a celebrated restorer of rivercraft. In medieval times the field beside the bridge grew hay to feed the King's deer in Richmond Park during bad winters.

Brooklands

Brooklands and the M25 are two much-discussed and, in some quarters, much-despised, circuits for motorists separated by more than eight decades. The great concrete ring constructed in the Surrey countryside near Weybridge by Hugh Locke-King was either loved or hated, and the same can be said of the M25, London's ring-road, or orbital motorway which, in spite of the impression given in the photograph, is often a nose to tail traffic jam as it cuts through Surrey from the Kent border to Heathrow Airport.

Locke-King, the grandson of Lord King, who built Brooklands House in 1822, was a motoring and aviation enthusiast, who in 1907 had the idea of bringing these two new passions on to the one site. With no shortage of willing hands, he constructed the two mile track in quick time, and soon huge crowds were flocking to witness great feats of derring-do both on the ground and in the air. Brooklands became a byword for speed.

When the track closed at the start of the Second World War, the aviation side was continued by names as famous as Barnes Wallis, who will always be remembered for developing the bouncing bomb featured so dramatically in the film, *The Dambusters*, and George Edwards, whose wartime engineer-ing skills were brilliantly employed in peace-time through the design and construction of Concorde.

Today, the Brooklands spirit and atmosphere survives thanks to an enthusiastic society dedicated to preserving the name. A section of the steep banking has been restored and is used on club days when owners of old and not so old, but nevertheless special, cars like to put their foot down to the floor and experience a thrill that sent a tingle up the spine of competitors and spectators alike 60 years and more ago. A museum in the original clubhouse is open to the public.

Shere

The Norman church of St James in Shere is tucked in behind the buildings on the east side of Middle Street, and beside the Tilling-bourne, the stream that is such a feature of the village. Shere acts as a magnet to visitors, and although the provision of a bypass to the north 30 years ago has removed the menace of through traffic, its narrow streets continue to be choked with the cars of people who come, ironically, to enjoy the peace of the countryside.

The Bray family has long been part of the fabric of the village and there are many memorials to various members in the church. William Bray, in 1801 when he was 65, took on a task most people would shrink at. Having joined the Rev Owen Manning in a colossal task to research the county for a major tome on its history, he found himself on his own when Manning died. But rather than quit, Bray took up the mantle and finished the job before he passed away, aged 96, in 1832. *History of Surrey* by Manning and Bray continues to be much in demand by today's historians.

Another member of the family founded the Anti-Litter League in an attempt to keep the countryside tidy. Regrettably, those visitors to Shere and anywhere for that matter, who drop their sweet papers and their ice cream wrappers and their fast food boxes and their cigarette butts from out of the ash trays in their cars, show not the slightest interest in the work of a pioneer.

The illustration on this page is of Holm-bury Hill, which is in the parish of Shere, and at 857ft above sea level is among the highest points in the county. In the museum at Guild-ford are artefacts found in the 1930s which came from a Stone Age camp on the hill.

Ewhurst

Tucked away to the east of Cranleigh, you could be forgiven for thinking that Ewhurst was on the road to nowhere in particular. It is, however, a busy little village: much more so than when the Victorian writer, Louis Jennings, came upon it in the 1870s and set down his findings in his marvellous book, *Field Paths and Green Lanes,* so long out of print but well worth hunting for in secondhand shops. 'I went forth into the village,' he wrote, 'which is sufficiently well described as a one-horse place. I met two or three persons only in the street, and they seemed to be half asleep. At the post office, a woman and a girl turned out in some consternation to look at me, thinking perhaps that I had a letter concealed about me, and was about to post it, and thus overwhelm them with work. A waggoner passed by on a load of hay, fast asleep. I too began to feel drowsy, and hastened towards the windmill which makes so prominent a feature in the landscape in all the southern part of Surrey.'

This is not the Ewhurst of today, and Jennings, were he to return, would be surprised at the change. The windmill, too, is long gone, converted into a house after it was closed in 1885. It would have been a prominent landmark for William Cobbett also, when he made one of his Rural Rides through Hampshire and Surrey in April, 1823. 'I treated my horse to some oats, and myself to a rasher of bacon,' wrote the Farnham-born man of many talents. He then headed off for Ockley through 'the deepest clay that I ever saw . . . I was warned . . . but I was not to be frightened at the sound of clay. It took me a good hour and a half to get along those three miles. Now, mind, this is the real Weald, where the clay is bottomless.'

Polesden Lacey

One of the several substantial National Trust properties in Surrey, Polesden Lacey also houses the organisation's regional offices. It is a fine building, dating from 1823, and on the site of a house which Sheridan, the politician and dramatist, bought in 1797. The new property was designed in the Regency style by Thomas Cubitt, and for more than 80 years it nestled happily and unobtrusively in

the rolling mid-Surrey countryside, given protection by the North Downs, climbing over Ranmore Common.

Polesden Lacey came alive in 1906 when it was taken over by Mrs Ronald Greville, a hostess with impeccable connections whose guests included royalty. The Duke and Duchess of York (later King George VI and Queen Elizabeth) spent part of their honeymoon there.

The house and 1000-acre estate were given to the trust in 1942, and now visitors can enjoy the place, whose gardens owe much to the work of Sheridan nearly 200 years ago.

At Leith Hill, which is shown on this page, the trust owns the highest point in the county. The summit is 967ft above sea level and is crowned by a tower, the top of which is at an altitude of 1000ft. It was built about 1765 by Richard Hull, who lived at Leith Hill Place, and when he died seven years later he was buried beneath his folly. The views to the South Downs and the sea are breathtaking, and it was recorded in the 19th century that 41 of London's church spires were visible from the summit. Much earlier, John Aubrey reckoned he saw all the home counties with the naked eye, and Wiltshire with the aid of a telescope.

Sandown Park

There are four racecourses in Surrey – at Sandown Park, Kempton Park, Epsom and Lingfield. Epsom, of course is the best known, and arguably the most celebrated in the country because it is the home of the Derby on every first Wednesday in June. Sandown Park is alongside the old A3 just a short walk from the centre of Esher, and its grandstand, situated on a hill, affords fine views not only of the racing but of the distant and increasingly suburban landscape.

While racing is the best known activity at Sandown Park, others, including conferences, dinners and auctions, keep the place busy. Esher town no doubt derives income from the racecourse, but its name alone has a certain affluent ring to it. Always the centre of considerable wealth, Esher and its hinterland, which includes the exclusive St George's Hill estate, appeared to be little affected by the recession of a few years ago.

It was one of the great stopping off places on the Portsmouth Road, and the Bear Hotel, in front of the old parish church, offered comfortable accommodation in the golden age of motoring. The Bear, although changed, still looks down on to the High Street which, in spite of being rid of its status as a trunk road, is still a busy thoroughfare.

The National Trust owns the gardens and lake at Claremont, just outside the town centre, and describes them as a microcosm of the 18th century English landscape garden, the *jardin anglais*. Sir John Vanbrugh built a house there in 1709 on what was known as Chargate Farm, and two years later he sold the property to Thomas Pelham, later the

Duke of Newcastle, who renamed it Claremont. Vanbrugh was given the task of changing his small house into a mansion, but after Pelham died in 1769 it was demolished, and the new owner, Lord Clive of India, built the present-day property which is now a school.

The River Mole

The stepping stones across the River Mole north of Dorking have fascinated visitors for nearly half a century. Few people will know of their history and, indeed, that they are not the original stones. This quiet and tranquil spot was first crossed by stones in 1932, but in no time at all they began to deteriorate. By 1946 they had been worn away to such an extent that they needed to be replaced. In their place were positioned much more robust stones which were better able to withstand the Mole's current.

The stepping stones carry thousands of pairs of feet every year on to and from the slopes of Box Hill. They were the gift of James Chuter Ede, MP, the Home Secretary of the day who had attended a local school, and they were declared open by none other than the Prime Minister, Clement Attlee, whose family connections were in the area now known officially as Mole Valley, and whose previous MP, Kenneth Baker, was once the Home Secretary.

The Mole is a lovely river that meanders for 42 miles through Sussex and Surrey before entering the Thames at Hampton Court. Nowhere is it more delightful than when it flows through the Mole Gap beside the great escarpment of Box Hill on the North Downs. Here, the river passes the Burford Bridge Hotel where, when it was known as the Fox and Hounds, Nelson stayed the night before leaving for Trafalgar and where he took his leave of Lady Hamilton. Keats and Robert Louis Stevenson knew the inn as a place where they could find the peace they needed for writing.

Nowadays, the rush of traffic on the A24, which the Romans called Stane Street and forded the river at the spot now spanned by Burford Bridge, interferes with the beauty and tranquillity of the place.

Dorking

The old town of Dorking is an ideal base from which to explore the Mole Valley. Its main feature is the wide High Street with the high pavement on the southern side and the 18th century White Horse Hotel. Dorking has a traffic problem and while the coming of the M25 to the north has obviously taken some of the strain, the A25 continues to carry its fair share of vehicles.

The countryside hems in the town and it is only a short distance to Box Hill, and Ranmore and Holmwood commons. On Ranmore, the church is a landmark for miles around, and is the resting place of its builder, Lord Ashcombe, whose father, Thomas Cubitt, a carpenter, died in 1854 leaving £1 million made from a life in the building trade in London. Denbies was the home of the Cubitts, but now the estate is owned by a local businessman who has planted thousands of vines which grow well on the chalky south facing slopes. The Denbies label is prominent in wine circles.

The town crest features a five-clawed cockerel, a sign that Dorking has been known for its poultry for centuries, indeed since the time of the Romans. Defoe, who lived near the town, said 'Darking' market was the most famous in England for poultry, and while this is no longer the case, and the Dorking fowl is all but extinct, the memory lives on. Local people are sometimes referred to as Dorking Chicks, and the football club's nickname is The Chicks. Eric Parker said the true Dorking fowl was a large, well-feathered bird and walked on five toes.

The old custom of Shrove Tuesday football through the town has been a thing of the past for almost a century, but in its heyday it was a rumbustious affair started by the town crier at 2pm at the church gates and lasting for four hours. Shops were boarded up as the players booted the ball along the High Street, but in the end it just got too much for the constabulary who, with the assistance of the magistrates, had the fun and games stopped for good.

Box Hill

On a clear day the view south from the North Downs can take your breath away. There is a widespread panorama over the Sussex Weald to the distant South Downs and, if you are lucky, the Channel through the Shoreham Gap. It is a scene that has attracted visitors to Box Hill from around the world, and one that gives so much pleasure. A few miles to the south of it lies the equally attractive Leith

Hill, from where the photograph inset on this page of the National Trust's rhododendron wood was taken.

Box Hill rises to 400 feet above the River Mole, and its summit can be reached from a number of paths. Whichever one is taken, the way is never without interest. It is little wonder that when the internal combustion engine was invented Londoners in their droves were encouraged to drive out to Box Hill so as to enjoy the freshness of the air and the space of the Downs.

But Box Hill was known long before the motor car changed the way people lived. Jane Austen's Emma told Frank Churchill: 'We are going to Box Hill tomorrow: you will join us. It is not Swisserland; but it will be something for a young man so much in want of a change.'

Earlier still, John Evelyn, the diarist, whose descendants still farm in Surrey, gave a clue as to the origins of the name when, in 1655, he observed: 'I went to see those natural bowers, cabinets and shady walks in the box coppses.'

Brockham

Bonfire night on Brockham Green vies with the one at Chiddingfold as the biggest celebration of Guy Fawkes Night in Surrey. And like the one in the south west of the county, Brockham's attracts a huge crowd of onlookers whose cars block the roads for miles around. Building the fire is a work of art, carried out under the supervision of experts, and security is high as the day nears. Unlike at Chiddingfold, there is no record of the Riot Act having either been read or prepared to be read, although police officers have become increasingly concerned about the hazards created by many thousands of people wishing to get as near to the roaring fire as possible in the centre of the village.

This problem, albeit on a much smaller scale and with danger being posed by different sets of circumstances, was the reason why cricket disappeared from the village green. In Eric Parker's day, and indeed much more recently, there was a good standard of play on view, and the immortal Dr W G Grace once strode the turf, although it was not at Brockham that, having been dismissed early in his innings, he reputedly refused to leave the crease on the grounds that the spectators had come to see him bat and not to see him bowled out.

Christ Church, which dominates one end of the green, was built as a memorial to Henry Goulburn, who was Wellington's Chancellor and Peel's Home Secretary. It is part of a scene which annually attracts the judges' eye in the county's best kept villages competition, and one that has earned Brockham an award on several occasions.

Buckland

How many passers-by, when travelling west towards Dorking, have seen the ancient barn at Buckland and thought it was a church? At first sight this fine, old building, with its tower and running fox weathervane, does have the appearance of a place of worship, and indeed it *was* when the parish church, which is on the opposite side of the A25, was being rebuilt in 1860.

The barn, sitting prettily on the green behind the village pond and with attractive cottages to accompany it, is much admired as a centrepiece of one of the most scenic corners in all the county.

The church, which has a wooden spire, has 14th century timbers in the roof, but its greatest attraction is its 600-year-old stained glass window in the south chancel depicting Saints Peter and Paul.

Buckland has a pub on the main road which looks out across the Reading to Tonbridge railway line to the North Downs. While it might not be an inn to which you might drive for a quiet drink on a summer evening, there are plenty of alternatives like the Surrey Oaks at Parkgate near Newdigate (pictured). The pubs hereabouts are often hidden deep in the countryside, although few retain the rustic quality of only a relatively few years ago. Too many have become victims of commercialism, with breweries making money on the backs of customers still willing to pay inflated prices for their drinks.

The reappearance of the small brewery offering its particular brand of real ale owes much to the dedicated supporters of CAMRA which was formed almost 30 years ago, and to beer festivals such as those held annually in Dorking and Farnham.

Redhill

When the Brighton line came in 1841, Redhill began to take shape, and in a century and a half it has grown into a bustling town and the centre of trade and commerce for east Surrey.

Eric Parker gave it his seal of approval – over Woking, at least – when he called it a 'better sort of Woking', adding: 'You do not have to wait for nine minutes to three-quarters of an hour every time you come to Redhill.' Nowadays, the station is an important link for commuters travelling to London, and for Gatwick airport. The cross-country line from Reading to Tonbridge, which cuts through delightful Surrey landscape south of the Downs, links Guildford and Redhill in probably the only tangible way. The west and the east of the county have very little in common, and this is especially so since the opening of the M25 which has removed the need for motorists to grind their way through Dorking, Reigate and Redhill every time they wish to go to Kent.

Redhill's modern centre is bright and attractive, and the Harlequin Theatre is a popular venue for the arts. Near the village of Nutfield, the Redhill airfield was an important Second World War aerodrome with Battle of Britain fighters stationed there.

The neighbouring town of Reigate, where the photograph on this page was taken, is an altogether older place which grew out of a Saxon village. Priory Park is a cherished open space close to the town centre, and the site of a 13th century Augustinian priory, while the old town hall, which dates from 1728, sits squarely on the site of an old chapel with modern shops and offices round about.

Charlwood

One of the most unspoilt villages in Surrey is how Charlwood was described a century ago. The writer may have heard of Bleriot and the Wright brothers, but he could not have imagined that on Charlwood's doorstep would have been developed one of the world's busiest airports. Gatwick and its environs have changed the way of life not just in Charlwood but in towns and villages across a wide sweep of Surrey and Sussex.

Pioneer aviators could scarcely have known what their achievements all those years ago would lead to. Gatwick (which is now in West Sussex; Charlwood having fought successfully to remain in Surrey) has long been associated with flying, but ony in the last 25 years or so has the airport become such a byword for international travel.

Unlike villages which have been drowned by the building of a reservoir or have been rendered a no-go area by the requirements of military training, Charlwood remains. Not the unspoilt place it once was, but a community nevertheless. The view of the Half Moon public house and the church of St Nicholas is still recognisable from much earlier illustrations, and gives the impression of solitude.

Some say the best way to see Charlwood is from the air, but this is unfair. A walk around the lanes is very rewarding, and that way you can call in at the church and see the rare wall paintings uncovered in the 19th century.

Outwood

Windmills nowadays, thank goodness, are invariably in the safe-keeping of a preservation society or similar organisation. Rarely do they have a purpose in life other than to provide interest and entertainment for visitors curious to know more about how their ancestors lived and worked. The mill at Outwood, 400ft above sea level, had a younger partner until 1960 when its great age caused it to collapse. Outwood post mill was built at the time of the Great Fire of London, and was believed to be the oldest working mill in the country at the time of its retirement. The inhabitants of the hamlet are said to have climbed to the top and watched the capital burn. Sometime later, the brother of its owner built a black eight-sided rival. However, recessions were not unknown in the milling business, and there was not enough work for both, so the upstart became redundant, and eventually fell into disrepair.

Modern-day Outwood's visitors come to see the old mill, or to watch the cricket on a picturesque ground, or simply to enjoy the open space on the common, which was given to the National Trust in 1955. Those who rush past on the nearby M23 know nothing of this attractive setting.

Caterham

There are 11 local authorities in Surrey; nine are boroughs, two are districts. Tandridge and Mole Valley are the latter pairing and their civic leaders are chairmen, whereas the other nine are mayors. There was a Tandridge Hundred at the time of the Domesday Book, and there is a small village of that name to the south of Caterham and the M25 where there is a wonderful, much supported yew in the churchyard. It is also near to Oxted where the civic offices are located.

The district council emerged when the county was reorganised. Out went Caterham and Warlingham Urban District and Godstone Rural District councils, and in came the new authority. Traditional seats of local government across Surrey disappeared in that shake-up, and the 11 authorities, with the county council sitting above them, took over. Since then, local responsibility and accountability has taken on a new meaning, and employees who have worked on both sides of reorganisation hark back to the old days with fondness.

Caterham-on-the-Hill and Caterham Valley make up a busy community dominated by the North Downs and close to the Greater London boundary. Trainee guardsmen will know the area if they spent time at the hilltop depot, which was built in 1877. The arrival of the railway in 1856 led to a building boom in the valley. Prior to that the inhabitants had lived around the Norman church on the hill.

William T Palmer, in his delightful *Odd Corners in Surrey*, published in 1951, warned cyclists of the severe gradients in and around Caterham. They must expect collar work, he said. On Succombs Hill on the road to Warlingham the average gradient in its 690 yards was 1 in 4.5 with a maximum of 1 in 4, he warned, and added: 'This is far from being a healthy place for a cyclist.'

Lingfield

Racing folk will know Lingfield as the venue for year-round sport, because there is now an all-weather track as well as the traditional turf. Lingfield Park is south of the village and a few years ago celebrated its centenary. After four years of National Hunt racing, the track was developed for the Flat and has continued to be one of the country's most delightful little courses.

The racegoers who attend the meetings will be aware that Lingfield is in the midst of some pretty countryside. Although it is close to both Kent and Sussex, it is still very much part of Surrey. But it is so far removed from Guildford, the county town, and indeed Kingston, in whose royal borough the administrative headquarters are situated, that it is sometimes mistaken for part of either of those other two counties. However, Lingfield is by no means isolated and its railway station, together with the one at Dormans to the south, near the villages of Dormans Park and Dormansland, are used by commuters to the capital.

The church of St Peter and St Paul is one of the grandest in the county, and has been called, perhaps somewhat extravagantly, the Westminster Abbey of Surrey. There are many memorials to the Cobham family of the now ruined Starborough Castle. The first Lord Cobham built the castle; the second one, in his will in 1417, founded a college close to the church for a provost, six chaplains, four clerks and 13 poor persons. King Henry VIII closed it in 1544.

From the Hog's Back – Front Cover

Fields of oil seed rape and poppies sweep down the northern slopes of the Hog's Back between Farnham and Guildford. The chalky spine of the North Downs, which carries the A31 road, affords superb views throughout the year, with the vivid colours in the fields in late spring making a spectacular picture.

Erl Wood Manor – Back Cover

Erl Wood Manor was built in 1825-1826 by Sir Edmund Currey (nephew and son-in-law of George III) who was at that time the Comptroller of the Household of the Duke of Gloucester. Set in forty-seven acres of countryside, the house has been beautifully preserved and retains many decorative features of architectural interest with its panelled rooms and moulded pillars and ceilings. There are Adam-style fireplaces with unusual Wedgwood plaques and a grand staircase which sweeps down to the entrance hall.